NEAR EAST

EAST ASIA

3100 First writing in Mesopotamia

2600-2400 Royal Graves of Ur

2500 Indus Valley civilization arises in India

2372-2255 Akkadian empire; founded by Sargon

1792-1750 Hammurabi rules Babylon

1500 Indus Valley civilization falls to invaders

1450-1180 Hittite empire at its height

1500-1027 Shang dynasty in China

1200 Sea Peoples raid Mediterranean coasts

973 Solomon becomes King of Israel

1027-256 Chou dynasty in China

669 Assyrians conquer Egypt
587 Nebuchadrezzar of Babylon besieges Jerusalem
539 Persians conquer Babylonia

c 600 Early cities near river Ganges in India
563 Birth of the Buddha in India
551 Chinese sage Confucius born

334-332 Alexander the Great conquers the Persian empire

326 Alexander the Great invades north India
256-206 Ch'in dynasty in China; Great Wall completed
206 Han dynasty begins in China
111 Chinese armies reach north Vietnam
52 'Hsiung-nu' (known in Europe as the Huns) become subject to Chinese emperor

66 Romans conquer Syria and Palestine

GREAT CIVILIZATIONS

Ancient Egypt

Longman

Contents

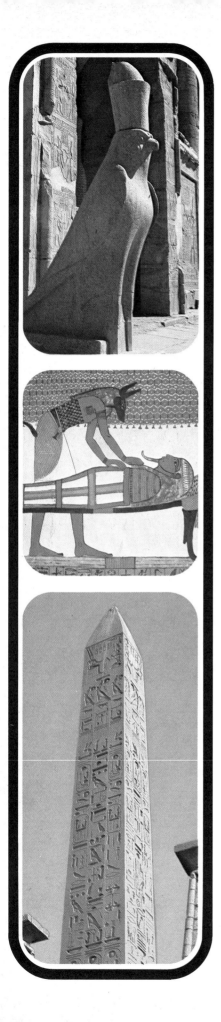

Left panel. Top: A statue of the god Horus, outside his temple at Edfu. Centre: Anubis, the god of embalming. Bottom: An obelisk, covered with hieroglyphic writing, outside the temple of Ramesses II at Luxor.

Editorial

Author
Anne Millard Ph.D.

Editor
Abigail Frost M.A.

Illustrators
Angus McBride
Brian and Constance Dear
Nigel Chamberlain

LONGMAN GROUP LIMITED
London

Associated companies, branches and representatives throughout the world

First published 1978

Designed and produced by Grisewood & Dempsey Ltd., Elsley House, 24–30 Great Titchfield Street, London W.1.

© Grisewood & Dempsey Ltd., 1978

Printed and bound by New Interlitho, Milan, Italy

BRITISH LIBRARY CATALOGUING IN PUBLICATION DATA
Millard, Anne
  Ancient Egypt. – (Great civilizations).
  1. Egypt – History – To 640 A.D. – Juvenile literature
  I. Title II. Series
  932   DT83

ISBN 0–582–39001–X

Ancient Egypt

Three things mattered above all to the ancient Egyptians – their king, the river Nile, and the Next World. Of these the Nile was the most important. For its annual flooding brought life to the desert and allowed plentiful crops to be grown. This freed Egypt from the risk of famine and made it rich. And so Egypt did not change much; it was so stable that its civilization lasted for 3000 years. Tradition was perhaps more important to the Egyptians than to any people since. Ideas, religion, and art styles were always based on what had been done before.

Just as the Nile died every year into a thin trickle but was soon reborn as a great life-giving power, so, each Egyptian believed, he would be reborn after death into a new and perfect world. The Egyptians were very happy on Earth, ruled by their pharaoh who was a living god. But they realized that perfection was impossible in life and hoped for it after death. The life they created for themselves on Earth, however, is full of fascination. In this book you will see how they lived, died, worked, played, and worshipped.

Above: A tiny pendant in the shape of a fish, made of sheet gold and green felspar. Egyptian jewellers were fine craftsmen in many materials.

Below: The 'Opening of the Mouth', the ceremony performed to enable the soul of a dead person to breathe and eat. Every Egyptian believed in a life after death.

The Beloved Land

For 3000 years a magnificent civilization reigned in a corner of Africa. Its people were surrounded by desert, but they were rich, comfortable, and well-fed. For this was Egypt, the land of the Nile.

Thousands of people every year visit Egypt and its monuments. What is it about the ancient Egyptians that captures the interest of so many?

One thing is the enormous length of time that Egyptian civilization lasted. From the first pharaoh to the conquest of Egypt by Alexander the Great is a longer span of time than that from Alexander to the present day. But for all those centuries the language, religion, art, and daily life of the Egyptians hardly changed. And the last remains of this culture did not disappear until well after Christianity had reached Egypt. We divide this long history into the Old, Middle, and New Kingdoms, separated by Intermediate Periods when Egypt was weak, divided, or under foreign rule. Within these, the *pharaohs* (kings) are grouped into *dynasties* – ruling families. A dynasty might last for several centuries or a few years.

The history of Egypt begins with a king called Menes, who united the country and became its first king. But it is not until the

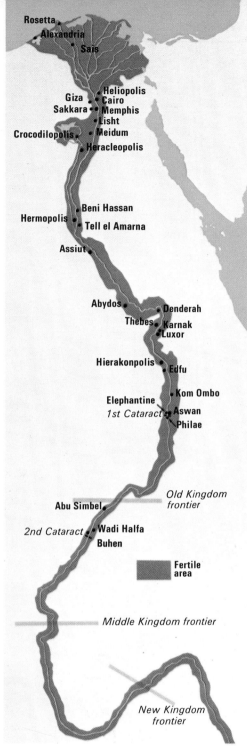

Above: The land of Egypt. The fertile land (shown in brown) is a narrow strip hugging the river.

Left: The pyramids of Egypt developed from a smaller type of tomb called a mastaba. Favourite courtiers were buried in mastabas. This mastaba belonged to a courtier of King Khafre, whose pyramid towers above it.

Right: Farming in the Next World, from a Book of the Dead. The Book of the Dead was a set of instructions to a dead person, telling him what to expect on his journey to the Next World.

Third Dynasty, which begins the Old Kingdom, that we can really be sure even of the names of kings. The great pyramids were built during the time of the Old Kingdom. It was followed by a time of disorder, when there were rival rulers in Upper (south) and Lower (north) Egypt. Egypt was re-united by a Theban prince, who founded the Middle Kingdom. It was a time of great prosperity, and Egypt began to build an empire. But new peoples were arriving in the Near East, forcing others from their homes. One, the Hyksos, took advantage of a period of weakness to conquer Egypt. At last the Egyptians rose up and drove the Hyksos out, and then began Egypt's most powerful age – the New Kingdom. But even the New Kingdom fell, to be followed again by foreign rule. Alexander the Great conquered it in 332 BC. After his death, Egypt was ruled by the family of one of his generals, Ptolemy. The last of the family was Cleopatra VII, and when she died Egypt became part of the Roman Empire.

The most amazing thing about Egypt is how much has survived from it. We can still look at great stone buildings and statues; tombs; reliefs and paintings showing daily life, wars, and worship; documents; and objects from people's homes. There are two reasons for this. The first is the hot dry climate of the country, which has preserved things that in many other places would long ago have crumbled away. And these objects were there to be preserved due to the Egyptians' great faith in a life after death. Many of their possessions were buried with them – all sorts of things that either were used in life, or represented things that were done in life. So we know about the lives of the pharaohs and their subjects.

CHRONOLOGY

ARCHAIC PERIOD
First Dynasty (c 3120–2890 BC)   Menes (Narmer?)

Begins with the Unification. Memphis founded as capital.

OLD KINGDOM
Third Dynasty (c 2686–2613)
Fourth Dynasty (c 2613–2494)
Fifth Dynasty (c 2494–2345)
Sixth Dynasty (c 2345–2181)

Egypt starts to become an important nation. Building of Pyramids. Trade with Lebanon and Nubia.

FIRST INTERMEDIATE PERIOD
The Seventh to the Tenth Dynasties (c 2181–2133). A time of great instability, whose history is not clear. Rival rulers in Upper and Lower Egypt.

MIDDLE KINGDOM
Eleventh Dynasty (c 2133–1991)
Twelfth Dynasty (c 1991–1786)   Senuseret III
Thirteenth Dynasty (c 1786–1633)

Egypt, united again, is rich and powerful. Trade with lands as far away as Crete. Senuseret III breaks the power of the over-mighty provincial governors. Thebes is capital as first, then It-towy (site uncertain).

SECOND INTERMEDIATE PERIOD
The Fourteenth (c 1633–1674: weak Egyptian rulers), and Fifteenth and Sixteenth (c 1674–1567: the Hyksos invaders) Dynasties. The Seventeenth Dynasty (at the end of the Hyksos period) consists of the princes who drove the Hyksos out.

NEW KINGDOM
Eighteenth Dynasty (c 1567–1320)   Hatshepsut
                                          Tuthmosis III
                                          Amenhotep IV
                                           (Akhenaten)
                                          Tutankhamun
Nineteenth Dynasty (c 1320–1200)   Ramesses II
Twentieth Dynasty (c 1200–1085)   Ramesses III

Egypt's great imperial age; its empire stretches from Libya to Palestine. Capital at Thebes. Pharaohs buried in Valley of the Kings. The 'Amarna Crisis' – Amenhotep IV imposes new religion and builds new capital.

THIRD INTERMEDIATE PERIOD
The Twenty-first to the Twenty-fifth Dynasties (c 1085–751). Egypt divided and weak, sometimes ruled by Libyan and Nubian kings.

LATE PERIOD
The twenty-sixth to the Thirty-first Dynasties (664–332). Periods of independence alternate with invasions. Egypt conquered by Assyrians and Persians.

PTOLEMAIC PERIOD
Alexander the Great conquers Egypt in 332 BC. Alexandria founded. After Alexander's death the Ptolemies rule, until the Roman conquest in 30 BC.

The Nile and its Gifts

The wealth, strength, and civilization of Egypt all were owed to the river Nile. It made the desert fertile. The Egyptians never forgot this debt.

In Egypt you can stand with one foot in a lush green field and the other in dry yellow sand. In the fields by the River Nile, the land is fertile, but beyond that is desert. Without the Nile, there would be no Egypt. This part of Africa would be as desolate as the Sahara Desert.

The Egyptians knew that they owed their existence to the river. They hailed Hapi, the god of the Nile, as 'The bringer of food, rich in provisions, creator of all good, lord of majesty'.

The Nile is the world's longest river, over 6400 kilometres (4000 miles) in length. It is formed from two branches, the White and Blue Niles, which join where the city of Khartoum now stands. Sometimes rocks come right down to the water's edge, and in six places rocks have actually spilt down into the river. These are the cataracts; fast currents swirl about the rocks and no ships can pass.

But most of the river runs through flat plains. These are the fertile lands of Egypt, but they are rarely more than a few kilometres across. Fertile space is so precious that Egyptian towns and villages are usually built on the edge of the desert. At Cairo the river divides again. Flowing to the sea through several channels, it has created the broad marshes of the triangular Delta.

Every year, when the snow melts in the Ethiopian mountains, enormous amounts of water crash down the Blue Nile. Before the building of modern dams, the land of Egypt was flooded for its whole length. This was called the Inundation.

The pyramids of Giza seen from the river. The lush green fields which feed the people of Egypt extend for a few kilometres at most.

Below: Egyptian fields were criss-crossed by a pattern of irrigation ditches. When the Nile was not in flood they were dammed. As the river began to rise, labourers broke down the dams and the water rushed in. This tomb painting shows such a ditch running among trees. The Egyptians always showed water by the zig-zag design seen here. The hieroglyphic sign for water was similar.

Real grain was used in this model of a granary to make it more true to life. Men pour the grain into the store-room through a hole in the top. A scribe keeps records to guard against theft. Models like this were placed in tombs to ensure that the dead man would have everything he needed in the Next World.

Because there is almost no rain in Egypt, farmers had to store the waters of the Inundation carefully. So they devised a system of canals, dykes, and basins to store the water and direct it into the fields when needed. The first sign of the floods came in June, and the water reached its height in September. Then it subsided, leaving behind rich black silt. This soil was so fertile it was sometimes possible to grow two crops before April, when the

A man uses a shaduf to water his garden. The shaduf was the first water-lifting machine invented. It was made of a beam balanced on a pillar. A bucket hung from one end of the beam, and a weight was fastened to the other. The user dipped the bucket into the river or irrigation canal. As that end of the beam was lowered the weight would rise. When the man let go, the weight would fall, bringing the bucket up. Then, with a swing of the bucket, the water was dropped into a ditch or over plants. This simple device is still used in Egypt today.

The farmer's year: In November when the floods had gone down, the seed had to be sown. Oxen dragged wooden ploughs through the black mud left behind. Then came the sowers, scattering seed from baskets.
Below: Paintings from a

hot season started. Then nothing could grow. Even the river began to dry up.

The Egyptian farmer's most important crop was wheat, for making bread and fattening cattle. Vegetables, including onions, garlic, beans, and lentils were also grown. Fruits included figs, dates, grapes, and pomegranates. But the Nile did not only provide food. Farmers grew flax to make linen. And along the banks grew the papyrus reed, used to build boats and to make 'paper'.

tomb showing farm work through the year.

Top: Taxmen measure the crop.
Centre: Reaping with wooden sickles.
Bottom: The threshing floor. Oxen are driven over the sheaves to drive out the grain. There might be time to grow another crop before the floods came. Then the farmers were called up to work on the king's building projects. In November they returned to plough again.

TAX DEMANDS

Money was not used in ancient Egypt. All the employees of the state — scribes, officials, workmen, and slaves — and the priests were paid in goods, usually food. This had been taken as a tax from the farmers, then stored until needed. The stores might also have to be used to relieve famine.

Tax officials measured the crops while they were still growing in the fields, and the taxes were assessed on their calculations. This system had the drawback that any number of disasters might happen to the crop after the assessment, but the tax demand went unchanged.

Right: Taxes in ancient Egypt were taken in food, livestock, or goods. Here the taxmen take away part of a farmer's flock of geese.

12

Pharaoh: King and God

The king of Egypt held absolute power in his country. He was a ruler, a general, and the chief priest of all the gods. He was also himself divine.

The pharaoh was thought to be a god – the descendant of the sun god. And the spirit of the hawk god Horus was held to enter into him as he sat on the throne with his royal regalia – the crown, the crook, and the flail. When he died, he became one with Osiris, the god of the dead. It was thought disrespectful to speak directly about this god-king, so people spoke of the palace as having done something. (*Pharaoh* – 'per-o' – means 'great house'.)

As the king was a god, an ordinary woman could not be allowed to share his throne. It became the custom for pharaohs to marry the only women who shared their blood – their sisters and half-sisters. Later other Egyptians began to imitate their kings and brother-sister marriages became common.

Each king had five titles. Three of them showed his godlike

Above: A carved palette found in Upper Egypt. King Narmer, wearing the white crown of Upper Egypt, is about to strike down an enemy. The hawk, standing on the reeds, is the hawk-god Horus. On the left is a servant carrying Narmer's sacred sandals. The King's name is written above, between the two horned heads of Hathor.

Tuthmosis III, the conquering pharaoh, with the great god Amun. The Ancient Egyptians believed that their pharaohs were gods on Earth, divine and all-powerful. This relief shows the close relationship between the pharaohs and the gods.

EGYPT'S FIRST KING

A priest called Manetho who wrote a history of Egypt in about 300 BC tells how Menes, a king of Upper Egypt, conquered Lower Egypt and so united the two lands. Manetho says that Menes ruled 62 years and was killed by a hippopotamus.

But who was this Menes? Since each king has more than one name, it is difficult to identify Menes among the known kings. Some people think that he was Narmer, who is portrayed on a palette celebrating his victory over Lower Egypt. One side shows him wearing the crown of Upper Egypt. On the other he wears the crown of Lower Egypt.

A relief from the temple of Ramesses II who is shown holding Nubian prisoners by the hair.

The feet of the mummy of Horemheb. He was an army officer who became the most powerful man in Egypt after the king during the reigns of Tutankhamun and Ay. Later he became pharaoh. Two bound captives are painted on the soles of the feet, showing how he trampled on his enemies.

A pharaoh, wearing the double crown, kilt, and richly coloured cloak decorated with embroidered feathers. The crook and flail show the care and power exercised by the pharaoh over his people.

nature. After came two names; one was the name he had had since birth, and the other was the throne name given at the beginning of his reign. The Egyptians never forgot that Egypt had been two separate kingdoms. In memory of this the king wore the Double Crown, made up of the White Crown of Upper Egypt and the Red Crown of Lower Egypt. The Crook and Flail were symbols of his authority. On ceremonial occasions the pharaoh (who was the 'Strong Bull' of Egypt) might wear a bull's tail attached to his belt. Pharaohs wore a false beard as a sign of masculine power.

The everyday running of the country was seen to by officials – the most important of whom was the vizier. They had great power, especially if the pharaoh was weak or a child. But the pharaoh was absolute ruler of Egypt. He owned the land and could do whatever he pleased with it. The pharaoh was also the chief priest of all the gods of Egypt. Everything, for the Egyptians, depended on him.

FAMOUS PHARAOHS

Senuseret III (1878–1843 BC) was one of the greatest kings ever to rule Egypt. Under the name of Sesostris he was still a hero of folk-tales over a thousand years after he died. This was because of the way he strengthened Egypt by military campaigns. He secured the frontier at the Second Cataract by building massive new forts. At home he broke the power of the nomarchs (provincial governors) whose authority had become a threat to the pharaohs.

Tuthmosis III (1504–1450 BC) left an inscription telling how an oracle chose him as heir to the throne (see page 29). But it is probably only a colourful piece of propaganda. After the death of his stepmother, 'King' Hatshepsut, he became one of Egypt's greatest warrior pharaohs. He fought a number of campaigns to win a large empire in Asia.

Tutankhamun (1361–1352 BC) was the king who restored the old gods. His reign was short and of little importance. But his name is

known more than any other pharaoh's today, because of his tomb which was found in 1922 by Howard Carter. It is the only royal burial to have been found un-robbed in the Valley of the Kings.

Ramesses II (1304–1237 BC) was a flamboyant warrior. Most of his battles were against the Hittites. Ramesses left an account of the battle of Kadesh in which he claims an almost single-handed victory: 'His majesty rode at the gallop and charged the enemies, having no-one with him . . . I found that 2500 enemy chariots in whose midst I had been were lying broken in pieces before my steeds'. But Hittite accounts make it seem that the battle was really a draw!

Left: a gold shrine from the tomb of Tutankhamun, showing the King with his queen. This is one of the many treasures found by Howard Carter in 1922.

Below: King Akhenaten with his wife, Queen Nefertiti, worshipping the god Aten.

THE QUEEN WHO WAS 'KING'

Princess Hatshepsut was the heiress to the throne of Egypt, and according to custom, she was married to her half-brother, the chosen heir. In 1512 BC he became pharaoh as Tuthmosis II. But Tuthmosis II died young, and was succeeded by his small son, another Tuthmosis. It was not long before Hatshepsut had pushed her step-son into the background, while she became pharaoh. This was extraordinary in Egypt, where women might have great influence, but only a man could actually rule. Yet Hatshepsut ruled successfully for many years. Her favourite minister was her architect, Senenmut, who built her mortuary temple – one of the most beautiful monuments in Egypt.

Above: A black granite statue of Senuseret III. He seems to have been an unhappy man. His statues are easily recognizable by his sad expression.

15

Life at Home

In town and country, the Egyptians lived in comfort. Their homes were well suited to the pattern of their daily lives, and the climate of their land.

The life of the Egyptian countryside. Irrigation makes it possible for the owner of this estate to use some land for a private garden – and to grow palm trees to shade his house. In the foreground labourers are preparing the soil for a new crop of vegetables. A house like this would be completely self-supporting in food, as well as producing grain for sale. This would be stored in the granary behind the house.

Modern Egyptian towns and villages are nearly always built on the ruins of ancient ones, so it is very difficult to find an ancient city to excavate. But a few settlements were abandoned and never rebuilt, and from these we have learned a lot about the homes of the ancient Egyptians.

All houses, from the peasants' hut to the most splendid royal palaces, were built of mudbrick. There might be door frames of stone, and columns of wood, if the owner could afford it. Poor peasants lived in one-roomed huts, but anyone who was better off would have a house with three sections. The outer room or group of rooms was for greeting strangers. The central room or group of rooms was for entertaining friends, and beyond this were the family's private quarters.

Windows were small and placed high in the walls at ceiling level, to keep the house cool. In the hot season everyone spent as much time as possible on the roof, where they would feel any cool breeze.

Noblemen's villas were very luxurious. They had many rooms – including bathrooms – outhouses, and gardens, all hidden behind high walls.

Country houses often had only one storey, but in cities, where land was

A tomb model showing brewers, bakers, and a butcher at work.

Above: A house belonging to one of the workmen who built the royal tombs at Thebes. These men lived in a specially built village in the desert. Most of the houses were in tightly packed rows, but must have been quite pleasant inside.

Below: The bustle of city life. A Syrian merchant ship is unloading at the quay. Egypt's best means of transport was the river, so most big cities were built beside it. Outside the narrow houses craftsmen have set up stalls to sell their work. The splendid temple is in the background.

A WOMAN'S PLACE

A woman in ancient Egypt could not hold public office (unless she was a powerful queen like Hatshepsut). But the legal rights of women in Egypt were better than in almost any other ancient society.

A father would usually leave most of his property to his eldest son, but daughters were also generously provided for. If a man had no sons, his daughters would inherit everything.

When a woman married, her husband might look after the running of her property. But it remained hers. She was entitled to make a will leaving it to anyone she chose. (In modern Europe, most married women did not have these rights until the late 1800s AD)

No woman had to endure a cruel husband, for divorce was easy. After a divorce, children would remain with their mother, and she and they were guaranteed shares of the father's property.

scarce and expensive, there were houses of three or more storeys. The main streets of these cities may have been magnificent, but the side streets were probably narrow, dirty, and teeming with crowds. Great cities like Memphis and Thebes were built on the Nile and had quays for shipping.

Craftsmen at Work

Egypt's craftsmen produced many wonderful things. Their work survives for us to admire in museums. But we know little about them as individuals.

Besides the peasants and the nobles, Egypt had a small but important middle class. Many of its members were the artists and craftsmen who made all the things that made life in Egypt comfortable. Some were craftsmen who made things for the local market. Others were employed in the workshops of rich patrons, attached to a temple, palace, or nobleman's estate. Often the patrons would have pictures of these workshops in their tombs, so we can see how the craftsmen worked.

Village of Craftsmen

On the west bank of the Nile near Thebes are the remains of the walled village of Deir el Medinah. It was built early in the Eighteenth Dynasty to house the workers who made the tombs in the Valley of the Kings. Today we can visit these men's houses, enter their temple, and climb the cliffs behind the village and examine the tombs they built for themselves. But an

Craftsmen at work making the things needed for a royal tomb. In the top row carpenters are working and a painter is decorating a shrine. Below them are metalworkers. Three are preparing a furnace; two heating it with foot bellows, and one stirring the charcoal. Below, two workmen remove a crucible full of molten metal with tongs. Other men are pouring the hot metal into rows of moulds.

even better insight into the lives of these and other Egyptian craftsmen comes from the many documents they left behind – written, not on expensive papyrus, but on *ostraca* (broken pieces of pottery).

There were usually about 60 men and their families living in the village. The men worked in two gangs, one on the left hand side of the tomb, one on the right. A few men actually cut the rock and the rest carried the rubble away in baskets. At mid-day the workers had a meal break. The working week was nine days long, with a holiday every tenth day. There were also holidays on religious festivals.

There was always a scribe in the village. His job was to see that the work was carried out according to the archi-

Some of the earliest Egyptians were craftsmen. This small frog, made of the much-prized stone porphyry, was carved some time before the First Dynasty.

This painting and the one opposite come from the tomb of the vizier Rekhmire. Rekhmire was in charge of the royal workshops and these are shown in pictures in his tomb. In the top two rows there are carpenters. Two of them are working on a bed with a bow-drill. This used the tension of a bow-string to spin a pointed drill. Below them is a man using a blow-pipe to raise the heat in a small furnace. Two other men smooth the surface of a large metal vase. Walking out of the picture on the left are three men carrying metals to be melted down. Two have baskets of small pieces on their heads.

A limestone statuette of a potter turning his wheel, from the Fifth Dynasty. The potter is shown realistically – he looks pinched and rather hungry.

THE FIRST STRIKES

Several times during the Twentieth Dynasty the workmen at Deir el Medinah were not paid on time. The food and other goods with which they were supposed to be paid did not arrive. After a while the workmen and their families were in real need.

Not surprisingly, the men went on strike. They marched to the temple where supplies were kept, and sat down outside calling for bread.

The workmen were able to get what they wanted by striking because it was unthinkable that the pharaoh's tomb should not be finished.

A headdress made for the princess Sit-Hathor Yunet, in the Twelfth Dynasty. It was found at Lahun with much other fine jewellery. It is made of gold, inlaid with semi-precious stones in rosettes.

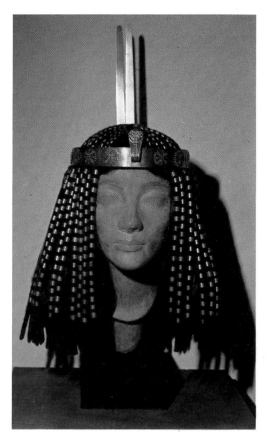

This glass fish is a bottle to hold cosmetics. It was made by winding rods of glass around a core to produce stripes. Then a point was drawn across the stripes to give the feathered effect. Its back fin is made of more rods left to harden in position.

Below: An inlaid box of wood and ivory. The Egyptians liked to use inlay as a way of improving the rather poor wood that grew in their country.

Ptah, the god who was the protector of craftsmen. He holds a smith's hammer.

tect's plans, and to keep a diary of the work. This recorded the issue of such things as lamp wicks and valuable copper tools and the excuses (often very thin) that the men gave when absent from work. The scribe made regular reports to the vizier's office.

The men were paid in goods – wheat for bread, barley for beer, vegetables, fats, oil, fish, cloth, and firewood. Sometimes there were special rewards from the pharaoh, such as wine, salt, natron (to be used as soap), and meat.

Once the cutting of the pharaoh's tomb was finished, artists moved in to decorate it. It is sometimes said that the men were killed to make sure that the exact position of the tomb remained secret. But this idea is completely false. We know from their own tombs that the men lived for the normal number of years. When they had finished the pharaoh's tomb they went on to make tombs for the queen and other members of the royal family.

Three gold finger-rings, all made from sheet gold and wire. The one on the right depicts a cat, symbol of the goddess Bast. The frog on the left-hand ring has a solid body and legs of wire.

Painters and Sculptors

Egyptian artists had no freedom to express themselves. Strict rules governed their work.

The Egyptians covered the walls of their temples and tombs with paintings and reliefs. The scenes inside temples show the daily services, and have enabled scholars to reconstruct the temple daily ritual. Scenes on the outside walls of the temple often show the achievements of the king, and these provide us with information about historical events. The walls of tombs are covered with scenes of daily life. These allow us a glimpse into the lives of ordinary men and women.

None of these scenes are there only for decoration. Tomb paintings are there as a way of taking care of the tomb-owner in the Next World. It was thought that everything in the painting would come to life if needed.

It was therefore most important that the artist draw everything according to the rules laid down by past generations. So no artist tried to show things in perspective, because that might cause the object to appear distorted. It was the custom to present the face in profile, showing only one eye. Both arms and legs had to be shown, and the chest had to be turned forwards.

Sculpture

The craftsmen who worked in stone used stone pounders, bow-drills, and copper tools. Even by the First Dynasty they were producing stone vases and dishes in the most amazing shapes in hard stones that are very difficult to work.

From the Old Kingdom onwards the Egyptians were also producing magnificent statues in stone, copper, bronze, and wood. Statues might vary in size from small figurines to colossal figures, up to 20 metres (60 feet) in height.

The Egyptians were capable of making fine portrait sculptures, but they did not always choose to do so. People chose to have themselves shown as young and handsome. That is how they wanted to be in their next life.

Above: A man making food-offerings. The food on the table is drawn without perspective, so that each item can be seen clearly. The man is standing in the conventional pose – chest full-face, head, hands, and legs in profile. His servants, less important than him, are smaller.

Below left: Colossal statues of Ramesses II outside the temple at Luxor.

Below: Another scene from the tomb of Rekhmire. It shows sculptors carving a large statue.

The Pyramids

The pyramids of Giza stand today, a symbol of ancient Egypt's might.

Visitors to Egypt have marvelled for thousands of years at the size and splendour of the pyramids. The group at Giza was one of the seven wonders of the ancient world – and most people still think of these pyramids as the 'Pyramids of Egypt'. Yet there are more than 30 royal pyramids scattered across Egypt and some 60 later royal pyramids in what is now the Sudan.

These spectacular monuments are tombs. Each pyramid was built to house the body and possessions of its owner.

Building the pyramid of Khafre. Some scholars think that a huge ramp was used to raise the stones. Hundreds of men dragged the stones to their position on sledges. But skilled workers were needed, too. In the foreground tools are being sharpened for masons who are finishing off the stones. A group of scribes are discussing the plans. Below the ramp the next sledges to go up are being loaded, so that the work can flow without delay. But most important in these gigantic projects was the enormous number of labourers needed – not slaves, but peasants unable to work on the land during the Inundation.

It guarded them and assisted the soul on its journey to the Next World. It also ensured its well being through eternity.

Pyramid complexes

Pyramid complexes vary a little according to their date, but most have some things in common. They were built on the west bank of the Nile – always in the desert, because all the fertile land was needed to grow food. On the edge of the cultivated land was the Valley Temple. Here embalming ceremonies were performed. A long passage – the causeway – led from this temple to the Mortuary Temple, which was built against the pyramid.

The pyramid's entrance was usually on its north side, well concealed. Inside it were a number of passages and chambers. The actual burial chamber might be in the body of the pyramid, at ground level, or underground.

As well as the king's pyramid there would be one or more small pyramids nearby. These belonged to the queen or to other favoured wives.

Old Kingdom pyramids were made of huge blocks of stone. These were brought from the quarry by boat up the Nile, then dragged from the river to the burial site by gangs of men. These men were not slaves but farmers who were used during the Inundation when work could not be done in the fields.

During the Middle Kingdom, kings were still buried in pyramids. These have not lasted as well as earlier ones, because they were made of mudbrick, with only an outer casing of stone. The New Kingdom pharaohs moved their capital from Memphis to Thebes, and changed their burial arrangements too. They were still buried on the west bank of the Nile, but in tombs cut out of the cliffs of a hidden valley. But they may have chosen this particular valley because towering above it is a rock – in the shape of a pyramid.

THE FIRST PYRAMIDS

Some people think that the pyramids grew from rectangular mudbrick tombs called mastabas. These were the burial-places of the earliest pharaohs and nobles. The outside walls had an elaborate pattern of alcoves, and inside there was a mound covering the grave.

Next came the Step Pyramid of Sakkara. This began as a stone mastaba, but there were two changes of plan while it was being built. The final result was a pyramid of six huge steps.

More step pyramids were built. At Meidum the steps of one were filled in, turning it into a true pyramid with smooth sides.

Above: After Egypt had been conquered by Alexander the Great, the rulers of the kingdom of Kush in Nubia continued some of the traditions of Egypt. These included being buried in pyramids. This group of pyramids is at Meroe, in the Sudan.

Top right: The Step Pyramid was built for King Zoser, who died in about 2950 BC. It is the oldest stone building in the world.

Right: The pyramids of Giza have been Egypt's greatest tourist attraction for many centuries. In the centre is the pyramid of Khafre, easily recognized because it still has some of its limestone casing. The largest of all, the pyramid of Khufu, looks the smallest because of the distance between it and the others.

Gods Great and Small

The Egyptians worshipped many gods. Some took bizarre shapes.

Osiris, lord of the Underworld.

The religion of the Egyptians may seem strange and complicated to us, but it served their needs for more than 3000 years. They worshipped many different gods and goddesses, and turned to them with all problems, joys, and sorrows. Many stories were told about the lives and deeds of these gods.

Egyptian artists often show the gods as animals or birds, or as men or women with animal heads. This does not mean that they thought the gods actually looked like this. Each god had an animal or bird particularly connected with him. Showing him with its head made him easily recognized, even by those who could not read.

One thing that confuses people today is that gods sometimes overlap – so there seems to be more than one sun god, and more than one god whose animal is a hawk. This is because in early times, before Egypt was one country, each area had its own gods and goddesses. These were still worshipped after the country became one, but some were not important outside their own areas. A god might be the protector of a particular city, for example. But other gods were important everywhere. The sun, which in Egypt dominates the sky nearly every day of the year, was one of the most important gods. The sun god's old names were kept as names for him at different times of day. He was Khepri, the scarab beetle, when he was reborn each dawn. At noon, in his full strength and glory, he was Re. In the evening he tottered to his death in the west as the old man Atum. Similarly there were many different hawk gods, but they all came to be united in the one figure of Horus, son of Isis and Osiris.

Osiris and Amun

Osiris was the ruler of the dead. The story told about him was that he had once ruled Egypt, with his sister Isis as his wife and queen. Together they

Right: A small statue of Amun, the great god of Thebes.

Below: The sacred boat of Amun, being carried in one of the processions that were a part of his festival.

Thoth, the god of wisdom and writing. He is seen here carrying the sacred sceptre in his right hand, and the Ankh, sign of life, in his left. As above, he is normally shown with the head of an ibis. At the judgement of the dead. Thoth was believed to record the result of the weighing of the dead man's heart.

Above: A bronze statue, with silver inlay, of the sacred bull of Apis, found at Memphis.

Above: A model of Isis, much-loved protector of children, suckling her son, Horus.

Anubis, the jackal-headed god, mummifying a dead man. When someone died, Anubis was believed to preside over the funeral.

Below: Taweret, the goddess of childbirth, was usually shown as a pregnant hippopotamus. She was a kindly goddess who looked after women and children.

helped mankind in many ways, and were greatly loved. Set, their younger brother, was jealous of them. He tricked Osiris into lying down in a beautiful chest, then slammed the lid shut, and sent it drifting down the Nile. The chest floated into the Mediterranean Sea and eventually was cast ashore at Byblos. After many adventures, the faithful Isis found the chest and brought it home. But Set was not beaten. He found the chest and cut his brother's body into pieces and scattered them in the river. Once more Isis set out. She collected all the pieces and joined the body back together again. Then, by magic, she restored life to her husband. He became lord of the Next World. Horus, the son of Osiris and Isis, defeated his uncle Set in battle. Then Horus was made King of Egypt.

In the New Kingdom, a new sun god became the most important of all. He was called Amun, and he had been the protector of the princes who had resisted the Hyksos. A grateful people identified him with Re. Amun-Re became the great state god, King of the Gods.

Scribes and Scientists

The best job in Egypt was that of a scribe. It brought security and power.

Above: A wooden model of a scribe, sitting cross-legged to write in a scroll.

'Behold, there is no scribe who lacks food ... The scribe directs the work of everyone else. He pays no taxes.' These powerful arguments were offered to the young people of Egypt by an old scribe recommending his own profession. Everything in Egypt had to be noted down for the records, so the scribe's job was bound to be important, secure, and well-paid. It was well worth the long hard business of learning to write – if you could afford it.

There were schools attached to palaces and temples. Rich men might engage a master to teach their children and those of friends together at home. A village scribe would of course teach his own sons, and perhaps those of neighbours who could pay him. The training was long, beginning when the boy was only four years old, and lasting until he was sixteen. Discipline was strict.

At first, a boy was not allowed to use papyrus, but had to write on *ostraca* (fragments of pottery or stone). He learned to write by copying out stories. Many of the great works of Egyptian literature have come down to us only as mis-spelled schoolboy exercises.

Once they had mastered writing, the boys in a school might go on to advanced studies. When he was fully trained a young scribe could rise to any heights, including even becoming a pharaoh's minister.

Practical science

Apart from history and religion, advanced study in Egypt was devoted to matters of practical use. The Egyptians would have

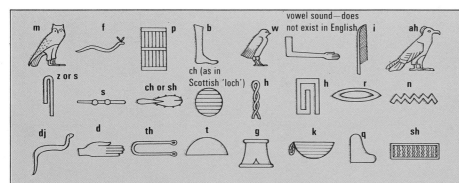

Above: The hieroglyphic alphabet.

Below: Stages in making papyrus. 1. The rind was removed and the pith thinly cut. 2. The strips were laid crosswise in two layers. 3. With a cloth on top, the papyrus was beaten with a mallet. 4. The sheet was polished with a stone.

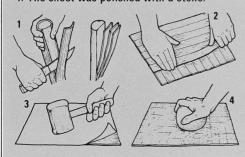

Below: The scribe's palette was a rectangular piece of wood with a slot to hold rush pens and holes for ink. Two palettes are shown here.

WRITING

The earliest kind of writing used in Egypt we call *hieroglyphs*. It is a script made up of picture signs. Some of these signs had the value of one letter of our alphabet, but others represented two or more. Words could be shown by a single sign, but most were made up of two or more. As well as these sound signs there were *determinatives* – pictures that came after a word to make you sure of its meaning. For example, after the sound signs making up the word for 'cat', a picture of a cat was drawn.

Hieroglyphs came into use about 3200 BC, and were still used on monuments and in religious texts after the introduction of Christianity.

thought it a waste to use their time worrying about what the mind was, or how matter is made up, as the ancient Greeks did later. First the people had to be fed and kept healthy, and enormous monuments had to be built. Astronomy may seem to be an exception to this, but it must be remembered that observing the stars was the only way for an ancient people to navigate accurately, or even to make a calendar.

The Egyptians were skilled mathematicians. They could do complex sums, including those using fractions. Schoolboys were often set problems, such as how much stone and how many men were needed to make a building of a certain size in a certain time. In geometry they could construct a right angle, and could work out the areas and volumes.

Although Egyptian medicine did sometimes involve using spells or prayers in the hope of curing disease, doctors had a very good knowledge of how the human body worked. Perhaps some of this came from centuries of embalming bodies. Some doctors were specialists, treating only one type of disease, or one part of the body. Egyptian doctors were famous for their immense skill throughout the ancient world.

The Sun's passage at night, shown in the ceiling painting in the tomb of Seti I. In astronomical drawings such as this the Egyptians showed the constellations as gods.

Below left: A mathematical text written in about 1600 BC. Egyptians used addition and subtraction to find the answers to problems which we would solve by multiplication and division.

Below right: A mummified hawk in a pottery jar, left as an offering for Imhotep, a great scientist of the Third Dynasty.

Above: Hieroglyphs from a wall relief of the Old Kingdom, describing the life of King Unas's son. We can see an oval frame drawn round several hieroglyphs; this denotes a royal name, and is known as a cartouche.

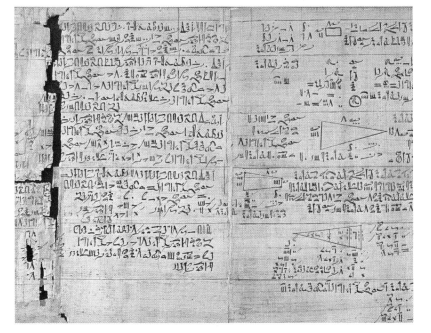

The Temple

A temple had to be a home fit for a god, and was built with a magnificence denied the homes of mortals. Priests dedicated their lives to looking after the god's daily needs.

Among the greatest buildings of Egypt are the New Kingdom temples. The most spectacular to have survived is Karnak, the massive home of Amun-Re, the King of the Gods. It covers a huge site in Thebes. Others, such as Luxor and Abu Simbel, are very impressive. The finest, however, is surely the temple built by Seti I at Abydos to honour Osiris. There in many rooms the colours still glow as freshly as the day they were painted.

The approach to a major temple was always impressive. An avenue of sphinxes led up to the pylon (ceremonial gateway), before which were obelisks, flag poles, and royal statues. A high wall ran around the temple, its sacred lake, and offices.

A temple was considered to be the house of the god, so, like ordinary houses, it was divided into three sections: an open courtyard, beyond which no common person could pass; a hypostyle (many columned) hall, where priests might enter; and the sanctuary, which was the god's private apartment. There were also side chambers where the objects used in the services were stored.

The daily ritual

Before dawn, the priests and priestesses on duty, having prayed and fasted, would purify themselves. Then they formed a procession which passed through the temple to the sanctuary. There, to the

The morning ritual in a temple of Amun. The chief priest has opened the shrine to wake the god and offer him food, incense, purified water, and flowers. In the shadows stand priestesses, who sing hymns. Each holds a sistrum – a musical instrument played by shaking. The priests and priestesses on duty lived in the temple, so that they were always ready to perform the rituals. Sometimes the king himself would attend, as chief priest of all the gods.

accompaniment of hymns and prayers, the doors of the sanctuary and the wooden shrine were opened to awake the god.

A religious service was not only an act of prayer and worship. The Egyptians believed that the gods needed food, shelter and clothing just as men did. All these necessities were provided during the course of the daily ritual. This was done by offering the statue pure water, incense, clothes, jewels, and food, so he could wash, purify himself, dress, and eat.

Besides visiting the temples, both great and small, the ordinary Egyptian kept many amulets to protect himself, and possibly had a small shrine in his house.

Hypostyle halls

Sanctuay

Pylon

Above: The main temple at Karnak had several halls leading to the sanctuary. The whole temple complex covers 32 hectares (80 acres) near modern Luxor, on the east bank of the Nile.
Right: A painted stone statuette of a priest. His wig has a 'side-lock of youth', a plaited lock hanging from one side. This was worn by boys until they reached adulthood, but was also worn by some priests.

ORACLES

The Egyptians believed that any god could come to earth, and his spirit could enter anything it chose — a man, an animal, a statue, rock, or plant. When it was on Earth like this, the god's spirit could answer questions through the creature or object it was occupying. So it became the custom to keep a sacred animal at the shrine of each god. At certain times, prayers were said and the spirit of the god might enter the animal, to give oracles — answers that revealed the god's will. Usually, the priest would ask a question which could be answered simply by 'yes' or 'no'. The animal could reply by, for example, eating from one of two food troughs. Once an oracle decided on the heir to the throne. The priests carried the statue of Amun-Re about the temple. When they reached one young prince, the statue became so heavy that they had to put it down. The god had chosen the next king, Tuthmosis III.

Egypt at War

The Egyptians could not simply enjoy their land without fear. The ancient world was full of shifting groups of people, looking for new territory to settle or conquer. The Egyptians had to keep them out – but sometimes themselves conquered others.

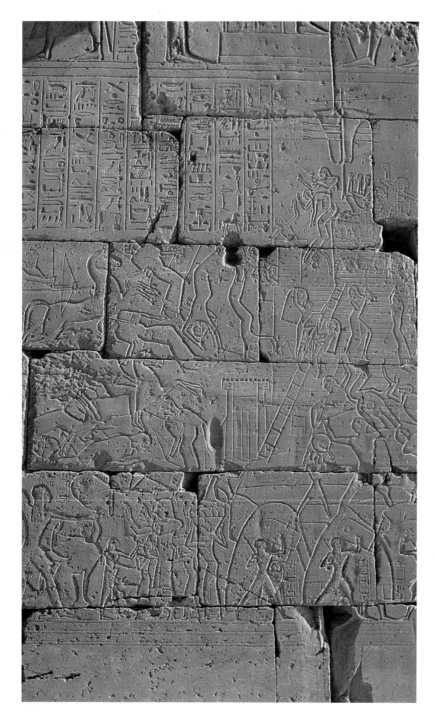

One of the duties of the king was that he should defend Egypt's frontiers and keep its people safe. Inscriptions have survived from the Old Kingdom telling of raids made across the frontiers to punish marauding Nubians, Libyans, and Bedouin. But no expedition aimed at conquest.

In the Middle Kingdom, however, their ideas changed and, in order to control the valuable Nubian trade routes, the Egyptians conquered Nubia as far south as the Second Cataract of the Nile. This brought them into contact with the war-like people of Kush. So they built a string of massive forts to guard their new frontier.

Later Egypt lost control of Nubia, and was itself invaded and conquered. The invaders were a people from across the eastern frontier, whom we call the Hyksos. The occupation lasted about 100 years. Then the Egyptians drove out the Hyksos and captured Nubia right up to the Fourth Cataract. They swept across Palestine and into Syria to gain a large empire.

Their success was partly due to the fact that they had learnt how to use the spectacular new weapon – the horse and chariot. The armies of the Old and Middle Kingdoms had been made up of lightly armed foot-soldiers. The armies of the warrior pharaohs of the New Kingdom were better armed and used at least some body armour. They included a division of chariots which could plough through the enemy foot soldiers.

Egypt's empire

The people of Nubia accepted the Egyptian way of life completely. This made things much easier for the Egyptians and left them free to work the Nubian gold mines. Egypt became rich

A siege scene from the New Kingdom. Soldiers, holding long spears and other weapons, are attempting to scale the walls of a city, some using long ladders.

with the gold from these mines. The people of the eastern part of the empire, however, kept their own ancient way of life and customs. To make sure they remained loyal, the Egyptians took the children of the local princes as hostages. The children were very well treated and were raised in Egypt to be loyal subjects.

The people of the empire had to send gifts regularly, which greatly increased Egypt's wealth. But there were neighbouring powers who wanted the Egyptians out of Syria. The Hittites managed to take over a large part of the eastern empire when Akhenaten ruled Egypt. He was too involved in religious affairs to take much notice of anything else. Later kings, such as Seti I and Ramesses II managed to stop the Hittite advance.

The last great warrior pharaoh was Ramesses III. He fought land and sea battles which saved Egypt from the Sea Peoples – an alliance of peoples from the islands of the Mediterranean – but, during the reigns of his successors, the empire was completely lost. Later kings dreamed of winning back the empire, but all their successes were short-lived.

DECLINE AND FALL

After Egypt had lost its empire at the end of the Twentieth Dynasty, it slowly declined. Nubian princes conquered Egypt, and were in turn overthrown by the Assyrians. At last Egyptian princes regained power, forming the Twenty-sixth or Saite Dynasty.

Then, in 525 BC, Egypt was conquered by the Persians. The Persians were so unpopular that when the Greek Alexander the Great invaded, he was welcomed as a saviour. When Alexander died, one of his generals, Ptolemy, took over Egypt. His family continued to rule for some 300 years. The last of these was Cleopatra, who killed herself after she was defeated by the Romans in 30 BC. Then Egypt became a province of the Roman Empire.

Tutankhamun driving his chariot, drawn by two horses, into battle – perhaps during a war against the Syrians. Chariots were introduced into Egypt by the Hyksos during their century occupation of Egypt, from 1674–1567 BC.

Two groups of wooden model soldiers, found at the tomb of Mesehti, prince of Assiut, dating from the Ninth or Tenth Dynasty. On the right are Nubians, holding bows and arrows, and on the left are Egyptians with spears and shields. The Egyptians relied on such foot soldiers until the beginning of the New Kingdom.

Trade and Travel

Egypt's great civilization was not isolated. Its wealth gave it great power in trading with other nations.

The soil of Egypt was so fertile that the Egyptians could grow all the food they needed, and still have plenty over for export. One text tells how, in time of famine, they sent grain to help their former enemies, the Hittites. Stone for building, semi-precious stones for jewellery, and copper and gold for tools weapons, and luxury goods could all be obtained from the deserts surrounding Egypt. The Egyptians exported articles as well as food; these included papyrus scrolls and ropes.

The one thing the Egyptians badly needed, but could not produce themselves, was timber. Egyptian trees, such as palm and acacia, give only poor quality, short planks. The area we call the Lebanon, however, grew great cedar trees, and these were exported to Egypt via the port of Byblos. Also from this area came resins, oils, silver, slaves, and, in the New Kingdom, horses.

From the earliest times, trade with Nubia was very important. It provided Egypt with slaves, copper, cattle, building stone, and amethysts. Beside these products, others from much farther south

One of the ships used during the expeditions sent by Queen Hatshepsut to the land of Punt. The oarsmen are rowing with long oars; square sails were put up when the wind was favourable. The Egyptians offered beads and trinkets; they took back with them ivory, ebony, gold, baboons, leopard skins, and precious myrrh trees.

THE LAND OF PUNT

Somewhere beside the Red Sea lay the land of Punt. Here there grew myrrh trees, which produced a gum which could be used as incense. (Incense is a substance which when burned gives off a thick scented smoke. No religious ceremony was complete for the Egyptians without it.) Today we do not know where Punt was; some people think it was south Arabia, others suggest Somaliland. Egypt sent expeditions to Punt from the Old Kingdom on; the most famous was sent by Queen Hatshepsut. This expedition brought back not only lumps of incense, but also living myrrh trees, so that the precious gum could be grown in Egypt.

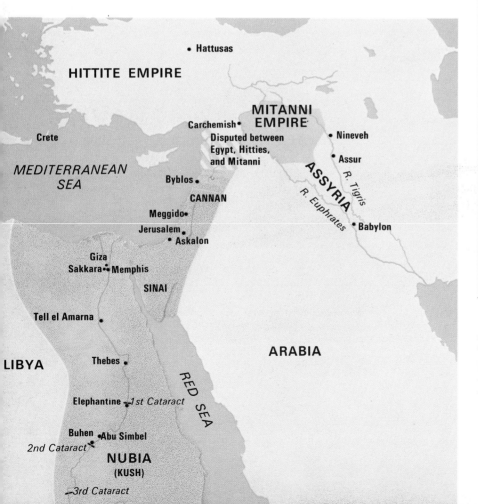

A map showing Egypt's empire after the Hyksos were driven out about 1570 BC. During this period, Egypt expanded her empire southwards to the third cataract of the river Nile, eastwards to the Tigris, northwards beyond Hattusas, and northeastwards almost to Greece, across the Mediterranean Sea.

passed through Nubia – ebony, ivory, incense, ostrich feathers, animal skins, and live animals. In the New Kingdom, to all these was added the most precious prize of all – gold, from the mines the Egyptians opened up in the Nubian desert. Unlike the people of the east, who retained their own religion, laws, and customs, the Nubians adopted a completely Egyptian way of life. About 730 BC, some 300 years after the Egyptians had lost control of Nubia, the king of that country marched north into Egypt to restore order – in the name of Amun-Re, King of the Gods.

Moving about

Good trade contacts are of little use unless there are good means of transport. Whenever possible, goods and people travelled by water. The Egyptians built a wide variety of boats, ranging from small papyrus skiffs, to wooden ships of many designs, and trading vessels that sailed in the Mediterranean and Red Seas.

When journeys had to be made by land, the rich had carrying chairs, borne on the shoulders of their servants. After the beginning of the New Kingdom, they might use chariots. Everyone else walked. Other wheeled vehicles were not used because no land could be spared to build roads. Light loads were carried on yokes over men's shoulders, or in panniers on donkey back. (The camel was not introduced to Egypt until the Late Period.) Heavy loads, such as building stone, were taken as far as possible by water, then put on sledges and dragged.

Envoys from Syria, presenting their tribute and paying homage to the king.

Left: Presentation of gold, mined in the Nubian desert, in the form of pieces and round-linked chains. Nubian gold was the source of much of Egypt's wealth.

Below: A light papyrus boat. Boats like this were used on the lower reaches of the Nile.

Death & its Rituals

Every Egyptian believed that he would enjoy eternal life after death. Tombs were supplied with furniture, food, clothes, and other things to keep the dead as comfortable as they had been in life. The dead were even given instructions on how to reach the Next World.

The judgement of Anhai, from a Book of the Dead. Anhai, led by Horus, has her soul weighed by Anubis a jackal-god, while Thoth records the result. A horrid creature waits below, ready to devour the unholy.

Throughout their history the Egyptians firmly believed that death was not the end of everything but the beginning of an eternal life. Seeing the effort that went into making pyramids and tombs, and the cost of decorating them, many people think that the Egyptians must have been a sad nation. Nothing could be farther from the truth. The Egyptians loved life and gaiety, and firmly believed that you could 'take it with you' to the Next World. It was only sensible, they thought, to put a lot of wealth and effort into making sure of a comfortable eternity.

There was of course a problem. You could not possibly take enough goods into the grave to last for ever. You could not even be sure that your relatives would go on offering food at your tomb. The Egyptians solved it by filling their tombs with models and paintings showing scenes of daily life – especially the growing and making of food. It was believed that if the right prayers were spoken, these scenes would come to life. Then the figures in them would work for ever to supply the dead man and his family.

Ideas of the Next World changed a little during Egypt's long history. In the early Old Kingdom it was believed that a dead king would join the sun god Re and sail across the sky every day in his holy boat. But by the end of the Old Kingdom, people began to believe that the king would become one with Osiris, the god of the dead. Egyptians of all ranks gradually turned to Osiris as their hope of eternal life.

PRESERVING THE DEAD

It was very important to the Egyptians that a dead body should remain in its grave as complete as possible. Otherwise the soul would be unable to return to it.

By the Eighteenth Dynasty an elaborate treatment had been worked out for wealthy Egyptians. In the embalmer's workshop the brain was drawn out through the nose with a wire hook. The internal organs were removed through a cut in the left side and preserved in the *canopic* jars — four covered jars made specially for this purpose.

Then the body was covered with a salt called natron, which dried all the moisture from it. This process took many days. The body was then washed and anointed with oils and fragrant ointments, and the empty space inside was packed with linen. Finally the body was wrapped with layer upon layer of linen bandages, and placed in one or more coffins. The whole process of mummification took 70 days.

We have a very good idea of what the Egyptians expected to happen in the Next World. They wrote it all in papyri and on the walls of tombs. The dead person would be ferried across the river to the kingdom of Osiris. There were many hazards to overcome, but the dead were helped by the *Book of the Dead*, a papyrus placed in the tomb. This gave a route to follow, spells for protection, and the right answers to any questions asked. At one stage the dead person had to face the Forty-two Assessors, who would ask questions about what sins he had committed.

Eventually the dead person reached the Judgement Hall, and was greeted by Horus, the son of Osiris. In the presence of Osiris the ceremony of the Weighing of the Heart was performed. Anubis, the jackal-headed guardian of the dead, weighed the dead person's heart against the Feather of Truth. A heart heavy with sin out-weighed the feather, and a terrible fate awaited its owner. A virtuous man would have a light heart, and pass on to a happy eternal life in the Next World.

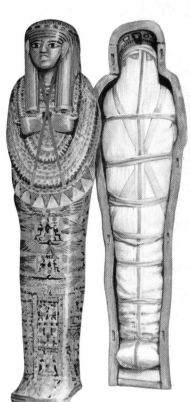

The mummy and coffin of an unknown priestess. Notice the carefully bound wrappings of the mummy, and the painting on the inside of the coffin.

The funeral procession of a New Kingdom pharaoh. A group of professional women mourners walks in front of a chest containing the inner organs pulled on a sledge. Four yoked oxen follow drawing the sledge of the funeral boat, in which rests the coffin containing the mummy. The royal standard-bearers accompany the boat.

Building

Egyptian builders had only simple tools. But they made up for them with ingenuity, careful planning, and their numbers – to produce some of the finest buildings of the ancient world.

A town house of mudbrick, with several storeys. Egyptian towns had many such 'skyscrapers'. This model was placed in a tomb, to provide a home for the soul.

Reconstruction of a reed shrine from the Archaic Period. Reeds are still used for elaborate buildings by the modern Marsh Arabs, who live in southern Iraq.

Many of the ancient buildings of Egypt fill us with wonder and surprise. Most surprising of all is the fact that they were built without the aid of cranes, pulleys, iron or steel tools, or wheeled carts.

The buildings we can see today are the ones the Egyptians meant to last for ever. A god or a dead pharaoh needed a house that would last. The living – even rich men or pharaohs – had houses of mudbrick.

The earliest Egyptians were hunters. They may have lived in tents. But as they learned to settle and become farmers, they built houses from the reeds which grew by the edge of the river. These developed into magnificent structures. The Marsh Arabs of southern Iraq have similar buildings today.

The early Egyptians then learned the art of making bricks. Nile mud and chopped straw were mixed together, shaped in moulds, and left to dry in the hot sun. This type of brick is well suited to the Egyptian climate, and is still used today in country districts there.

During the Archaic Period the Egyptians began to use stone. Houses of all kinds were still made of brick, but stone was now used for temples and tombs.

Building a temple
When the king had approved the plans for a new temple, orders went out to the various quarries to cut the right amounts of the different types of stone that would

be needed. The blocks of stone were loaded on to sledges, and large numbers of workmen hauled the blocks down to the waiting ships. The blocks were then floated as near as possible to the building-site. Then men and sledges took over again.

Meanwhile, the ground had been levelled, and the plan of the temple had been marked out on the surface. The foundations had been laid, and a foundation ceremony has been conducted, perhaps by the king in person. The first layer of blocks was then laid in place for every wall and column of the temple. When this was done, the spaces between the blocks were filled with sand and a

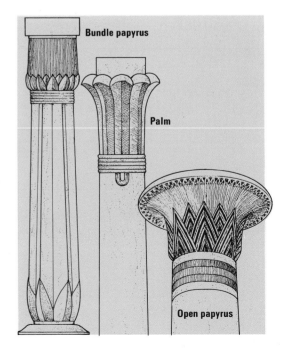

Bundle papyrus

Palm

Open papyrus

ERECTING AN OBELISK

How did the Egyptians cut the huge obelisks from the rock and set them in position?

This question has been partly answered by the discovery of an unfinished obelisk in a quarry at Aswan. This showed that the quarrymen had first cut a shallow slit in the rock. Then they drove wooden wedges into the slit, and poured water over them. This made the wood swell, and forced the rock to crack away from the quarry wall. Then the obelisk had to be detached underneath, smoothed, and decorated, and taken to the temple.

At the temple a system of ramps had been prepared, rising to the height of the obelisk itself. In the centre was a funnel. The plinth for the obelisk was at the bottom and the funnel was filled with sand. The obelisk was hauled up to the sand-filled funnel, then hauled into the upright position on top of the sand. A tunnel at the bottom of the funnel was opened and the sand removed. As the sand sank, the obelisk settled till it rested on its plinth. The ramps could then be removed.

short ramp was built outside. The second layer of stones was dragged up the ramp and across the flat surface of stone and sand. When the second layer was in place, more sand was put in and the ramp was lengthened. This process was repeated again and again until the roofing stones were in place. Then artists and sculptors moved in and began decorating the walls from the top downwards. As they completed each layer the sand and the ramp were gradually removed.

Below left: Columns from Egyptian temples are often designed to represent plants. Below: Similar columns in the hall of the great temple of Amun-Re.

Above: The unfinished obelisk. Right: The obelisk outside the temple of Ramesses II. Below: How an obelisk was put into position.

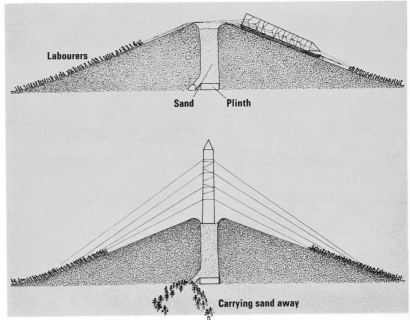

Labourers · Sand · Plinth

Carrying sand away

37

Clothes & Make-up

Egyptians took great pride in their appearance. They relished fine clothes, jewellery, cosmetics, perfumes, and wigs.

Egyptians, like most other peoples, suited their clothes to their daily lives. Both men and women wore loose clothes, as in many parts of the Near East today, in order to keep cool.

In the Old and Middle Kingdoms the usual dress for men of all ranks was the kilt. This would vary in length, reaching from waist to knee, calf, or ankle, according to the job, age, and rank of the wearer. Kings and nobles wore pleated linen, and leather or beaded belts with rich inlaid buckles. In the New Kingdom wealthy men wore a robe over the kilt.

A peasant woman doing heavy work might wear only a short skirt, but the usual dress for women was a simple tunic held in place by two straps. In the Old and Middle Kingdoms these dresses might be of white or plain coloured linen, or they could be patterned. Those who could afford them also had elaborate beaded over-dresses, while pictures of goddesses and queens show them in gorgeous dresses covered in feathers.

For much of the year Egypt enjoys a hot, dry climate, and children and those engaged in heavy energetic work did not wear any clothes, or wore only a brief loin-cloth.

Only linen cloth has been found in tombs, but, as they kept sheep, it is difficult to believe that the Egyptians did not use wool too. In tomb paintings almost everyone is shown dressed in white, but we know that coloured and patterned cloth was used. Garments found in the tomb of Tutankhamun were brightly coloured.

Above: Queen Nefertari, the wife of Ramesses II. As a queen, she wears a crown, but her fine pleated dress might be worn by any noble woman of the New Kingdom. Below: Amenhotep I, wearing a kilt and a pleated underskirt of fine linen. Bottom right: A tomb model of a weavers' workshop.

Above: A woman applies lip-paint with a brush.

Left: A woman of the Eighteenth Dynasty. She has long hair in many plaits or ringlets; this may well be a wig. Her eyes are outlined with black, and her brows are painted. She wears a headband and collar. Below: A collar and necklace made of flat moulded beads.

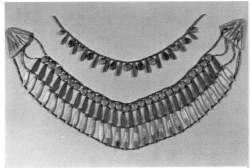

Cosmetics and hairstyles

Long before the Unification, Egyptians were already using eye paint. Both sexes outlined their eyes with a substance known as kohl. This was made of either malachite (green) or galena (dark grey) which was ground on palettes, mixed with water, and stored in special little jars until needed. It was applied round the eye with small sticks. Red ochre was ground and mixed with oil or fat to make lipstick.

Classical authors tell us that Egyptian perfumes were the best available. They were made by steeping flowers and other fragrant substances, such as aromatic woods, in oil and then wringing it through a cloth. The Egyptians also made cones of perfume grease. These were placed on top of people's wigs at banquets. As the grease melted and ran down the face, it was fragrant and cooling.

Egyptians liked elaborate hair styles. Sometimes the hair was short, but usually important men and women are shown with long thick hair. In the case of men it may fall around their shoulders, but women often wear it longer. Both sexes have their hair arranged in many small plaits, or in elaborate curls.

Not everyone, however, had enough hair of their own for these styles. Or they may have preferred to keep their hair short, because of the heat. In order to have the fashionable styles for important occasions they would either pad out their own hair with false locks, or would wear a wig. Whether made of wool, human hair, or other fibres, these large wigs must have been very hot to wear.

JEWELLERY

All Egyptians, men and women, wore a lot of jewellery, in a wide range of materials. Gold, silver, copper, semi-precious stones, inlays and glazes, a material called faience, shells, and attractive stones picked up in the desert were all used. These would be formed into many different pieces — circlets and diadems for the head, earrings, broad collars of beads, necklaces, pendants, armlets, bracelets, and rings.

Most of the Egyptian jewellery we know today comes from tombs. In spite of centuries of wholesale robbery, some wonderful pieces have survived to prove the supreme skill of the ancient Egyptian craftsmen. Special jewels and *amulets* — small objects thought to have magical powers — were made to be placed on the corpse and among the bandages of mummies.

Spare Time

On the sporting field and at home, the Egyptians enjoyed their leisure time in many different ways.

Daily life in Egypt was of course hard, especially for the peasants. At certain seasons farmers and their families had to labour in the fields from dawn to dusk. But there were slack times even for the farmers, when people had leisure to enjoy themselves. And there were public holidays – important religious festivals lasting several days.

Although the Egyptians did not have theatres or public games and races like the Greeks and Romans, they had some colourful and exciting public spectacles. As well as the many royal and religious processions, there were sacred dramas. These showed episodes in the lives of the gods, and were performed in temples each year by priests and priestesses.

Many of the sports enjoyed by the Egyptians grew up out of the needs of battle. Some pharaohs held displays at which they showed off their skills with horses and weapons to their troops. Reliefs in some temples show a kind of duel, where soldiers fight with wooden swords. Each has a narrow wooden shield strapped to his left arm, running from his hand to his elbow. Wrestling seems to have been popular. One Middle Kingdom tomb has a large painting of wrestling holds and throws. From the New Kingdom there are reliefs showing bare-fisted boxers.

A favourite sport of boatmen was a water tournament. Two teams assembled in their boats, armed with long poles. The object of the game was to knock your opponents into the water without losing your own men. Another river sport was swimming. This must have been risky in some stretches of the Nile where crocodiles and hippopotamuses were common.

Above left: A 'cartoon' showing a gazelle playing a friendly board game with its enemy the lion. Possibly the loser gets eaten. These board games were very popular.

Above: A nobleman and his family on a fowling trip. The man is using a stick to knock down the birds while his wife holds him steady. The family cat may be there to act as a retriever. More likely its job was to frighten the birds and make them fly up out of the reeds.

Below: Tutankhamun and his hounds run down two ostriches. This object is a fan-mount. Once (like the fan on the left of the decoration) it held ostrich feathers, which is probably why the artist chose to show this subject. The ostrich, no longer found in Egypt, can run very fast, so the chase would have been long and exciting. It was thought very proper for a pharaoh to excel in the hunting-field, and Tutankhamun's chariots, bows, and arrows were all buried with him.

A banquet in a private house. Guests might be entertained by singers, musicians, acrobats, or dancers. All food was eaten with the fingers.

Hunting was popular. It was not only a sport for the Egyptians. Desert animals, such as gazelles and hares, were hunted for meat. But noblemen enjoyed chasing more exciting game, such as lions and wild cattle. In the Old and Middle Kingdoms animals had to be stalked on foot and attacked with bows and arrows and spears.

There was good hunting on the river as well as on land. Nobles went after waterfowl with boomerangs and after fish with spears. Crocodile and hippopotamus hunts were more exciting.

Private pleasures

But most of the Egyptians' amusements were private. A day on the river was often a family outing. One painting shows people having a picnic afloat. Those Egyptians who did not care for active games could choose from a number of board games. The pieces and boards for these were often beautifully made. One game involved two set of pieces, one with heads of hounds, the other with jackal heads.

Music and singing gave the Egyptians a lot of pleasure. A favourite theme of tomb painting is a banquet where musicians entertain. Musicians played harps, lutes and other stringed instruments. Singers were sometimes accompanied by a group of musicians, and harpers might sing as they played. Dancing was another favourite entertainment at banquets. As well as listening to professionals, many Egyptians liked to make music themselves. The Egyptians particularly liked parties.

Reading, for some, was a favourite pastime. There were many stories to choose from. The most popular (judging from the number of copies that still exist) was the story of Sinhue. This was the tale of a young soldier who everheard a state secret, and fled to Syria in fear of his life. He had many adventures, and at the end of his life was invited back by the pharaoh. But only a few could read these stories – others would listen to storytellers.

Children's toys found in Egyptian tombs.

PLEASURES OF CHILDHOOD

Children of the ancient world often had to work hard. In Egypt, many had to help in the fields. Girls were taught household skills, such as cooking, weaving, and spinning, by their mothers. They also had to look after younger brothers and sisters. Boys had to learn farming or a craft. Even the children of the rich had to learn skills such as writing. But in spite of all these duties, children still found time to play.

Egyptian children had many toys, some with moving parts. A small girl buried at Lisht owned a set of carved ivory dwarfs, on a flat base. By twisting a knob at the side, the dwarfs can be made to twirl as if they are dancing.

Below: Musicians performing at a banquet. The girl on the left is playing a double pipe, her neighbour has a lute, and the last girl is a harpist. Her harp could be tuned by means of pegs. Each girl wears a cone of perfume on her head.

Glossary

Archaic Period The time between the Unification and the Old Kingdom — the First and Second Dynasties.

Amulets Small magical objects, which the Egyptians believed would ward off evil spirits.

Book of the Dead A papyrus scroll of instructions and prayers, placed in a tomb to assist the dead man on his perilous journey to the after-life.

An amulet in the shape of an eye.

Canopic jars Four jars in which the internal organs of the body were preserved to protect them for the after-life. The lids were shaped like animal heads that were symbols of the four sons of Horus, who were the special guardians of these parts of the body.

Demotic The last and simplest version of the Egyptian written language of hieroglyphics. It was developed around 700 BC.

Dynasty A succession of rulers of the same family. For example, the Ptolemaic dynasty were the descendants of the ruler Ptolemy.

Embalming The process of preserving a body by soaking it in oils and spices. Beforehand, all the body's liquids have to be dried out.

Heretic Somebody who believes in a different idea or religion from the one most commonly accepted.

Hieratic A simplified form of hieroglyphic used in the Middle Kingdom.

Hieroglyphic The written language of the Egyptians. It consisted of picture symbols, sometimes representing words, sometimes consonants.

Hyksos A Western Asiatic people who invaded Egypt from the East. The Hyksos ruled for 100 to 150 years. It is thought that they introduced the horse and chariot to the Egyptians. They were expelled eventually by the princes of Thebes.

Hypostyle hall The central hall of an Egyptian temple, which had many columns.

Inundation In Egypt the period from June to September was a time when the Nile flooded. Waters from the Ethiopian mountains poured into the Nile. It rose and over-spilled its banks, depositing a thick layer of fertile silt on the land. When it had receded, the Egyptians began planting their crops. In modern Egypt, great dams control the Nile's waters to prevent flooding.

Kohl The eye-paint used by the ancient Egyptians and some Near Eastern people today. It was usually black or green. It was made from a variety of stones. These were ground into powder and then mixed with water. Kohl was worn by both sexes.

Late Period The Twenty-sixth to the Thirty-first Dynasties. The time when Egypt was conquered by the Assyrians and Persians, but had some periods of independence.

Lute A musical instrument, played by plucking strings with a pick.

Mastaba A type of tomb, used from the Archaic Period onwards. It was built of brick or stone.

Memphis The capital of the Old Kingdom. Memphis was situated a little above the modern Cairo on the west bank of the Nile. The pyramids stand very close by. Very little remains today.

Middle Kingdom The Eleventh, Twelfth, and Thirteenth Dynasties, dating from 2040 to 1633 BC.

Mummy The remains of a body, after it had been dehydrated with natron, covered in preserving oils and spices, and wrapped in tight bandages. It would then be placed in a coffin and sarcophagus (an outer stone coffin).

Natron A drying chemical used by the Egyptians to remove all the moisture from a body so that it could be mummified.

New Kingdom From the Eighteenth to the Twentieth dynasties, covering the period from 1567 to 1085 BC.

Nubia The land beyond the First Cataract in the south was known as Nubia. In the early days, there was peaceful trade between the two countries.

Obelisk A monumental pillar, erected outside Egyptian temples. Obelisks were made from a single piece of stone. The tip might be gilded to catch the rays of the sun god Re in the morning.

Old Kingdom The Third to the Sixth dynasties, from 2686 to 2181 BC.

Ostraca Fragments of pottery or stone used for writing less important documents. Children's lessons or simple calculations were written on ostraca.

The well-preserved 'Papyrus of Hunefar'.

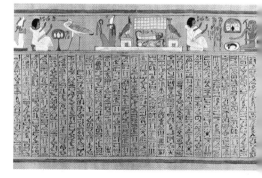

Papyrus A reed that was very common in Egypt. Papyrus was used by the Egyptians for making paper, and also light boats. The word can also mean a document written on papyrus.

Pharaoh The king of ancient Egypt. Pharaohs were also regarded as gods.

Pre-dynastic period The period before the Unification of Egypt.

Pshent The double crown of Upper and Lower Egypt. The White Crown of Upper Egypt was high and conical. The Red Crown of Lower Egypt had a curious high back. Together they showed the unity of both parts of the Kingdom.

Ptolemaic Period The 300-year rule by the descendants of Ptolemy, who was a general of Alexander the Great. The dynasty ended with Cleopatra VII, who committed suicide when the Romans invaded in 30 BC.

Punt, the land of The land somewhere by the Red Sea, with which the Egyptians traded to buy incense and myrrh trees.

Rosetta Stone The famous slab of stone discovered by Napoleon's soldiers during his campaign in Egypt. It was inscribed with the same text in hieroglyphics, demotic, and Greek. The brilliant scholar Jean-Francois Champollion first deciphered hieroglyphics with its aid.

Scribe One of the officials who

The Rosetta Stone, which gave the key to Egyptian hieroglyphic writing.

wrote things down, and acted as record keepers. They oversaw public works and recorded public occasions.

Sphinx A mythical beast with the head of a man and the body of a lion. The most famous is the Great Sphinx at Giza. It has the head of King Khafre.

Thebes Capital of the New Kingdom, on the east bank of the Nile, Thebes became a magnificent city. It was the centre of worship for the sun god Amun. The temples of Karnak and Luxor, some of the most magnificent of all Egypt, were close to Thebes, and can still be seen today.

Unification The time when Upper and Lower Egypt were first united as one kingdom, in about 3118 BC.

Valley of the Kings The barren valley which the pharaohs of the New Kingdom chose for their burial site. Their tombs were cut into the rock of its cliffs.

Vizier Most important of all the Pharaoh's ministers. A vizier was rather like a modern prime minister.

SOME GODS AND GODDESSES

Re The sun god. Although the Egyptians had many other sun gods, Re was the name generally used.

Amun-Re The great state god of the New Kingdom. Amun had been a local god of Thebes, and was merged with Re after Theban princes expelled the Hyksos.

Aten The disc of the sun — the single god whose worship Akhenaten tried to establish in place of the other gods.

Osiris The god of death and rebirth. The story of how he was

murdered and restored to life symbolised the rebirth of the harvests and of man.

Isis The wife of Osiris and mother of Horus.

Horus Son of Isis and Osiris. The pharaoh was thought to be Horus on Earth.

Anubis The jackal-headed guardian of the dead. He performed the 'weighing of the heart' when the soul of a dead man was judged.

Hathor A mother goddess, in charge of music, dancing, and love. She was represented in the form of a cow.

Horus, Osiris, and Isis – a small statue from the Late Period.

Index

Bold entries indicate a major mention.
Italic numerals indicate an illustration.

ACKNOWLEDGEMENTS

Half title, Michael Holford; Contents page, Michael Holford, Ronald Sheridan (centre); Page 7 British Museum (top), Ronald Sheridan; 8 Michael Holford; 10 Robert Harding Associates; 11 Michael Holford (top), ZEFA; 12 British Museum/John Freeman (top), Michael Holford (above centre and right), Ronald Sheridan; 13 Peter Clayton (top), Michael Holford; 14 Middle East Archives (top), Michael Holford; 15 British Museum (top), Michael Holford (right), Peter Clayton (bottom); 17 Michael Holford; 18 Robert Harding Associates (top), British Museum; 19 Robert Harding Associates (top), Oriental Institute, University of Chicago; 20 Peter Clayton (top centre and top right), British Museum (right centre and bottom right), Michael Holford (left); 21 ZEFA (top), Michael Holford (bottom left), Peter Clayton; 23 ZEFA (left), Michael Holford; 24 British Museum/John Freeman, Middle East Archives (bottom centre), Michael Holford (top right); 25 Michael Holford, Ronald Sheridan (bottom left); 26 Louvre, Paris; 27 Robert Harding Associates (top), Michael Holford, Middle East Archives (bottom); 29 British Museum; 30 Robert Harding Associates; 31 Peter Clayton (centre), Middle East Archives; 34, 36, 37 Michael Holford; 38 British Museum (bottom left), Peter Clayton; 39 Robert Harding Associates (top left), Peter Clayton (top right), British Museum (centre); 40 British Museum (bottom), Ronald Sheridan; 41 Michael Holford (top right), Middle East Archives; 42 Michael Holford; 43 British Museum (centre), Louvre, Paris.

Picture Research: Penny Warn and Jackie Cookson.

EGYPT	EUROPE

BC
3118

3118 'Menes' unites Upper and Lower Egypt

2686-2181 Old Kingdom

2650 Death of Zoser, for whom the first pyramid was built

2181-2040 First Intermediate Period

2040-1633 Middle Kingdom

1878-1843 Reign of Senuseret III

1633-1567 Second Intermediate Period; includes the Hyksos period

1567

1567 Hyksos driven out

1567-1085 New Kingdom

1504-1450 Reign of Tuthmosis III, who wins a vast empire

1379-1362 Reign of Akhenaten, who tries to change Egypt's religion

1179

1179 Ramesses III defeats the Sea Peoples

1085-751 Third Intermediate Period

669 Assyrians invade Egypt

525 Persians invade Egypt

332 Alexander the Great invades Egypt

31

31 Romans under Octavian defeat Cleopatra VII (Egypt's last queen) and her husband Mark Antony. Egypt becomes a Roman province

---

3000 New Stone Age in northern Europe

2000 Stonehenge built in Britain

2000-1900 Greek-speaking tribes enter Greece

1650 Mycenaean civilization in Greece

1500-1300 Bronze Age in northern Europe

1150 Dorians invade Greece

1100s Phoenician colonies in Spain
900s Rise of Etruscans in Italy

900-750 Rise of Greek city-states

509 Founding of Roman Republic

336 Alexander the Great becomes King of the Greeks

44 Murder of Julius Caesar
36-30 Struggles for rule of Rome between Mark Antony and Octavian